The SECRET WIVES

NIKIYA MONE

Copyright © 2021 Nikiya Mone

All rights reserved. No part of this publication may be reproduced, distributed, or transmitted in any forms or by any other means, including photocopying, recording, or other electronic or mechanical methods, without the prior written permission of the publisher, except in the case of brief quotations embodied in critical reviews and certain other noncommercial uses permitted by copyright law. For permission requests, write to the publisher, addressed "Attention: Permissions Coordinator," at the address below:

Nikiya Mone

P.O. Box 5299

East Orange, NJ 07019

DEDICATION

Who would have thought that three years later, I'd be telling the complete truth about the "Secret Wives." This book is dedicated to my unborn baby, whose heart beat its last beat on 4/24/2018. As a woman, when you learn you have conceived the way I learned, to lose your baby after feeling every sickness due to the pregnancy hormone, you crave for that feeling just one more time. I have yet to have that one more time so I will cherish the memory of you and how proud and happy I was to be carrying you.

This book is dedicated to every woman who has lived in secret with a man only to discover the game was being ran on you. This book is dedicated to every man, who has been broken by an already broken woman who didn't know how to love herself, adore herself and cherish herself. This book is dedicated to every child that has had to grow up too fast because adults couldn't understand how to put them first. This book is dedicated to everyone who can relate to the raw emotion expressed throughout the chapters. This book is dedicated to the one person who helped me to heal in the third year, to show me with actions and words what it meant and felt to be loved and loved without having to lose myself. He's been a true confidant, a real friend, a trusted advisor, and a true keeper. Dieudonne Merceus, I truly cannot thank you enough for all you have done for simply believing in me beyond what I could even see. To my sisters, Jessie and Nadiyah; you two have been my rock, and my sanity on days when I didn't think I could go on. My niece and nephews have been my lifeline. Christopher, Jayson, Xavier, and Lily, the children I never had, you guys have been my "children" in place of my inability to birth my own.

Lastly, this book is dedicated to ME! You made it, Nikiya Mone! You have finally made it! You've made it to freedom, you've made it to wholeness, and you've made it to your due season at the appointed time.

CONTENTS

Dedication III

1 - Suffering Loss 1

2 - The Meeting 7

3 - To Believe Or Not To Believe? 16

4 - I Cannot Fail 23

5 - Deep Cover 32

6 - The Secret Wife 58

7 - Is It Adultery? 74

8 - The Trauma 87

9 - Bigamy In The Church! 115

10 - Journey To Freedom, Fearlessly! 137

1

SUFFERING LOSS

When I was a little girl, I dreamt of one day being married and having children. I wanted to be around people whom I loved unconditionally and vice versa. I wanted a big wedding and all my family and friends there to witness me become the Mrs. However, those dreams were far from my reality.

The truth is as a child, I was taught to dream big; stopping at nothing to get what I wanted. I was taught that the sky's the limit. So, I soared academically and professionally but personally, I couldn't climb. I went from one dead-end relationship to the next without accomplishing or reaching the desired end result: marriage, children, and happiness. Instead, I was constantly hurt, upset, feeling used and abused, whether physically, emotionally, mentally, and/or spiritually. I never could master long-term, committed relationships.

There was a running joke amongst my parents and sister with whether my relationships would last 90 days, 120 days, or more. Most didn't make it past the 90-day mark. For years that was my benchmark to determine whether the relationship was solid enough to be considered worthy of moving forward.

I started dating at sixteen, and from the age of sixteen until now, my parents have only met five men that I considered serious enough to bring home. Even they couldn't withstand the true test. In spite of that, I never gave up my hopes of becoming a wife, mother, and homeowner.

In July 2007, I embarked on a self-discovery journey. I cleaned up my life and started going to church. I started a quest to find my biological father. I was working in Pennsylvania, and I knew my biological father was from Pennsylvania. I decided to use Google to locate him. I was able to find him by contacting my grandparents. They gave him my number to contact me. I hadn't seen my grandparents in about sixteen years.

When my father called, he and I spoke for hours, catching up on each other's lives. I remember telling him that I dated men exactly like him. He asked me what I meant, and I told him that he used women to meet his needs, whatever those needs were. I attracted men who needed my help so much that I put their wants, needs, and feelings before my own. During that conversation I became aware of my issue and since then, I've been fighting to overcome my battle with codependency.

After years of failed attempts in relationships and not finding the love that I wanted, in August of 2016 I thought all of that had changed. My aunt lost her battle with Ovarian Cancer. To watch someone who was so full of life, slowly but quickly deteriorate right before my eyes hurt badly; it honestly broke me. In the weeks leading up to her passing, I remember her calling me in to her room when we were the only two home.

She said to me, "Kiya, I don't want to die. Pray for me."

And I prayed right there. I prayed at church, I prayed everywhere; hoping and praying that God would turn her diagnosis around, praying that God would perform a miracle and surprise the doctors and my aunt and show them how real He is. I prayed that He would heal her and manifest His power on the earth. I prayed and prayed and prayed and prayed until they were taking her out the house into the hospice in order to get her pain medicine under control. As they were taking her, her boyfriend and I were trying to make sure that she had everything she needed.

She snapped at us, saying, "Ya'll act like I'm not coming home. I'll be back. I'm just going there to get my pain meds under control."

I loved my aunt. She was like a mother to me, so to lose her hurt. I was devastated; I was broken. Her passing broke me emotionally and spiritually. I felt God didn't heal her because of something I did or didn't do. I felt that I had failed her because there was a prophet who wrote her name on Facebook and said he needed to speak to someone named Sharon, and I reached out to the prophet and said I have an aunt named Sharon who was sick and in the hospital.

He said, "I need to speak to her right away."

When I reached the hospital, my aunt was asleep. She was having trouble resting due to the amount of pain she was in, so I waited, and I let her sleep. When she woke up, I asked her if she would speak to the prophet, and she said she would. However, we were never able to connect via the phone due to her health deteriorating and her constant battle of being sick.

After her passing the guilt of why I didn't force the issue of her speaking to the prophet hit me hard. Maybe if I had, like Hezekiah, maybe she would still be alive today. I felt guilt and shame and I became angry with God for not healing my aunt. I felt like all I asked was for one thing, for God to manifest His glory, to release His healing power and He didn't heal her here on earth. My aunt passed and I lost the person who was always there for me no matter what. The guilt I carried after her passing was extremely heavy, and due to the guilt, hurt, pain, and anger, I started back drinking heavily in order to mask the pain.

How do you lose someone who was so pivotal in your life, someone who was always there for you, someone who you could count on? How do you process the loss of someone such as her and there is no replacement?

2

THE MEETING

I can remember the very day when I met him. It was a hot summer day on July 7, 2016, and I was invited to go to a church service in the Bronx, NY. I can remember driving around the block a few times because there was absolutely no parking. I finally found a parking spot a couple of blocks away from the church.

When I walked in the church, there weren't a lot of people there yet. I took a seat in the second row from the front, close to the aisle. The church quickly began to fill, and prayer started. The guest preacher wasn't there yet. However, some people came in that I knew from New Jersey.

I can remember a young lady walking in and sitting behind me. She left her seat and, when she did, the people from New Jersey sat where she had been seated. She asked me if she could sit in the row with me, and I moved over to make space.

Then a man walked into the pulpit and took his seat. I thought to myself, *This is the guest preacher? The bishop?*

There was a young man with him and I noticed someone else who walked to the organ. He was introduced and my first thought was how old is he to be a bishop. He had a jovial look and a young, innocent smile and the two young men who were with him seemed very young.

As the service progressed, he preached briefly, then moved into the flow of the prophetic. When someone moves into the flow of the prophetic, they are supposed to be hearing from God and giving you the word

God is speaking to them concerning you, a situation, a condition, but the word spoken should be specific to you. When he began to minister to the people in the prophetic, the young lady began to assist him by standing behind or to the side of the people he was prophesying to. It was at that time that I realized she was part of his ministry team, along with the two young men.

He prophesied to a lot of the people in the service; then he prophesied to me and spoke life and healing into me. And for the first time since my aunt's passing, I felt alive. That night something happened spiritually that I hadn't felt in a long time; it was almost like a spiritual awakening. After the service was over, he and his ministry team retreated; I assumed to the back office. When he came out from the back, the only two people with him were the two young men. I didn't see the young lady again. He shook everyone's hand, then he leaned in and shook my hand, and kissed me on the cheek. I thought it was strange, but I didn't give it any more thought.

About a little over a month later, on August 20, 2016, I saw him again at another service in Queens, NY. The same young man from the Bronx, NY service was there with him. There was also an older woman, an apostle, there with him. She was not the same woman at the service a month earlier. Bishops often travel with different members, so I thought nothing of it. It depends on the availability of the members of their ministry teams. I later learned that the young man was always there because he was his armor bearer.

It was an extremely hot August summer day, and the service was running well overtime. The air conditioning could hardly be felt with the amount of people that were in the small storefront space. The woman who came with him had left, so I thought, and he asked for something to drink. I offered him a ginger ale because that was all they had left at the church to drink.

However, the ginger ale was extremely hot due to the conditions in the church and it was not refrigerated. Because of the hot ginger ale, from that day on, he called me his five-minute wife because I offered him a hot soda on a hot day. We laughed about it and exchanged social media information. For a period of time, we spoke via private messenger before exchanging phone numbers.

After I met him and we exchanged phone numbers, I did a background check on him to see what would come up. What I saw was that he was, in fact, divorced from who I would later find out was his first wife. I saw a tie-the-knot registry for the second wife. However, I didn't see a divorce record. So I texted him and asked him if he was married. He immediately called me and asked me why did I ask him that. I told him whenever I meet someone, I will perform a background check on that person; and what I couldn't find was a divorce record for his second wife as he stated that he was divorced. He told me emphatically that he was definitely divorced; that as a man of God all he had was his name, and how he protected his name at all costs. He advised that he had a good name, and he intended on keeping it that way; so yes, that he was divorced.

One night we were on the phone and he asked me if I was in a relationship with anyone. At the time I wasn't exclusive with anyone and I told him that. He told me to stop speaking to the man I was dating. He told me the Lord showed him what the man was doing and advised that I leave that man alone quickly. He told me he was a real man and wouldn't play with my emotions and that God brought us together and I didn't need to be found any longer, because he had found me. From there, we started dating.

After the passing of my aunt, I stayed at her house for about three months. For the first two months of our relationship, he would often visit me at my aunt's house in the city. At times, he would bring his armor bearer with him and we would laugh, talk, and eat. At times I would cook.

One night, while speaking, he started calling out numbers, and the numbers he called out "happened" to be my aunt's date of birth. When I advised him that was my aunt's date of birth and that she had passed away, he began to describe my aunt's facial features, the glasses she wore, and even her voice.

He spoke in such a way; I was in awe and immediately was in tears because I had missed my aunt so much. He shared with me that as a prophet of God what he was about to do was not allowed, but he sensed that I needed closure. So, he told me that he heard a voice, a woman's voice, and this voice was calling my name.

He then described my aunt and said she wanted me to know that she was okay. He also told me to let my grandmother and my mother know that my aunt was at peace and that everything was going to be fine; for us not to be upset. He advised that by her birthday, I'd be receiving something as that date was significant.

However, I never shared that information with my grandmother or my mother. I wasn't comfortable with relaying that type of message to them. However, I listened and felt comforted knowing that she was okay. Naively, I thought, *Surely, this must be a man from God, whom God sent.* Why would God provide such detailed *information to someone that He did not send?* Almost immediately, the co-dependency began.

The Secret Wives

3

TO BELIEVE OR NOT TO BELIEVE?

Towards the end of August 2016, he had accepted a ministry assignment in California. When he went to California, we didn't speak much while he was out there. We went from speaking almost every day, all day, to barely a few words. So, I had become frustrated. His armor bearer called me via FaceTime and flipped the camera to show him laying across the bed fast asleep.

The musician made a comment, which I found extremely disrespectful. I asked the armor bearer why he was calling me and not him. The musician said something to the effect of, "Because he doesn't want to speak to you."

As a grown woman, I was not accustomed to dealing with outside people. I hung up the armor bearer, texted him, and told him that I was done.

He acted as if he didn't know what was going on, apologized, said it wasn't intentional. He was extremely exhausted due to the time difference and had no idea his armor bearer even called me. At that point I told him no longer would allow anyone else besides him to call me when it came to us. I was not friends with his armor bearer or musician, and he respected that for the most part.

When he returned from California, he called me because we were supposed to go to dinner. He was in New York City, and his armor bearer was in the Apple Store purchasing an iPad. When he called me, he began to explain to me why we couldn't go to dinner. He told me how embarrassed he was about it because one of his members had called and needed help with bills. She was a young mother and, as a pastor, if his members were in need, he had to help them out.

In addition, upon returning from California, he was met with an extremely high parking bill from the airport. He had parked in short-term parking instead of long-term parking. He didn't make as much money going to California as he had anticipated since he didn't believe in setting an honorarium. He always expected the inviting church that requested for his gift to do right by him.

So, of course I understood. He was a pastor, a bishop, helping a young mother in need, a member of his church. Of course, I understood ministry assignments and the possibility of the inviting churches inability to pay an honorarium; giving what they could without pressing on the pockets of the people. I understood why, at that moment, we could not go out to dinner. I offered to cook for him, but I told him that he could NOT bring his armor bearer with him; not that time. He respected my wishes.

As time passed, I asked him why he always travelled with his armor bearer, even during personal times. He advised that he kept the young man close to him to protect him; like a father would protect his son. I thought that was admirable. Even though he was only three years older, the armor bearer referred to him as "Dad." I never questioned the relationship. I could understand needing the protection of your spiritual parent; someone to watch over you not only spiritually but also naturally.

The depth of his manipulation was bottomless. He had a way of presenting himself as the protector, provider, and father. He acted as if he was generous and never received back what he gave out. He made it seem like others always abandoned and left him broken. He told me how he lost his churches due to the cost of the divorces from his first and second wives. He was always the one who had to walk away with nothing. Those revelations about him stunned me because I could relate to those feelings.

There was a time when he was having car troubles, and I offered him the use of my car. He would drive my car to his home in Rhode Island when he needed to rest. He claimed he had an apartment in Rhode Island where he lived by himself, but since he was always traveling on the road, all he would do was pay the bills.

On a few occasions, he offered to take me to Rhode Island because I had never been there. In the beginning, I never went. At one point, he told me that he was placing all of his belongings in storage. It was a waste of money to pay rent for a place he hadn't been consistently living in for over a year.

No matter the story, I believed him. Why would he lie? I also allowed him to drive my car to Ohio to see his daughter and attend his preaching engagements. Apparently, the car trouble he had was outstanding parking tickets. Later, I found out that his car had no insurance or registration because he had no license due to all his unpaid tickets. Nevertheless, I understood everything and didn't question it. Who hadn't experienced issues with parking tickets?

The Secret Wives

Nikiya Mone

4

I CANNOT FAIL

In September of 2016, he began having services in Asbury Park, NJ. He advised me that he was originally having services in Trenton with great turnouts at Friday Night Fire services. He wanted to establish services every Sunday in Asbury Park, NJ. One Sunday, I decided to drive down to the church service in Asbury Park from New York City.

It was there that I saw the young lady, and the older woman that I had seen previously at the other services in New York. I also met another woman there as well;

along with a group of teenagers who attended the services. At the end of the services, he would always walk me out to my car. Then he would go to the other women's cars to ensure everyone was safe. I honestly didn't think anything of it. It was a ministry with women and teenagers, small enough for him to be personable and ensure the safety of those under his covering.

During a visit to my aunt's house with him and his armor bearer, I asked him about the women in the church. Specifically, about the two that I had seen previously at the services in New York.

I asked him if he was dating them, and he stated, "They wish I was dating them."

He advised the young lady was far too young for him to ever date. However, she wished she could have him. And he stated the older woman was far too old for him. But, it appeared she wanted a young man because she would always attempt to bring him dinner.

I didn't think anything of those statements. In ministry, when there is a young, single pastor, let alone a bishop, it is common practice for women to attend the ministry with the hopes of possibly dating/marrying the pastor/bishop. He reiterated for me that he was with me, so again, I didn't have a second thought about it.

It was on September 25, 2016, on a Sunday. I had purchased two tickets to go to the Bad Boy Reunion Tour. I was supposed to go with my friend's son, but it was also the same Sunday that he was officially launching the church in Asbury Park, NJ.

I thought about going to the concert over supporting him at the launching of his church in New Jersey, but I decided to go to the church service as opposed to the concert.

I contacted my friend's son and advised him both tickets were his; then I got ready to go to church.

As I was driving to the church, it was a sunny day in September. I was driving across the George Washington Bridge from New York City to Route 80 to get on the Garden State Parkway to drive down to Asbury Park. Suddenly, I grew sick and felt nauseous. I had to pull over on the highway to throw up. I chalked that up to me eating too many sweet potato chips. An officer pulled up behind me to check to see if I was okay. Once I assured him that I was fine, he pulled off after me.

I still headed to the service, determined to support him at his official launching of the church. When I arrived, he acted thoroughly surprised and happy to see me there. I sat in the back of the church and spoke to others politely.

The young lady I had seen at the Bronx, NY service asked that I move up to the front of the church. I obliged out of respect. It was there that I was sitting next to the other woman, the older apostle that I had seen in August on that extremely hot day at the Queens, NY service.

The official launch service was nice; I started to go to his church regularly every Sunday. He asked that I take over the administrative function of the church; he didn't have anyone that was capable of handling that aspect. It was at that time that the warfare began. The young lady and I were able to get along pretty well; we worked well together. However, the older woman was another story.

As I began to create certain documentation, standard communications, etc., everything became an issue and a need for discussions regarding who was responsible for what. Apparently, there was some overlapping of responsibilities.

The older woman and I did not get along. One day he contacted me and came to my aunt's house, looking and appearing to be in distress. He appeared to have not slept or even showered. He rushed to me because the older woman was spreading rumors about me and tried to warn him against having me as a part of the ministry.

He then created a series of videos for all of us to watch. They were created while he was in his car outside of my aunt's building. I was sitting next to him as he recorded them. The videos were to admonish anyone from speaking or spreading negativity, amongst other things. After everyone was done viewing the videos, they were to respond affirmatively with their understanding.

Immediately following the release of the videos, the older woman contacted him, and I could hear her apologizing and asking if she had done anything wrong. This was all on a Saturday. The next day at church, the same older woman came to me as I was in prayer to apologize to me. I felt someone's hand on my back. The words that she used to attempt to assassinate my character had me extremely angry, and one thing I didn't like to be was angry in church. So, I went into prayer to remove my anger.

Later, I found out that when he noticed her coming to me, he had sent his armor bearer to watch what was going on.

This was the first sign of many signs that I ignored as it pertained to what was going on within the walls of the church. After that incident, things didn't get better in the church; things got worse.

After one service, he had a meeting with us in the downstairs area of the church. It was in this meeting that he officially established our roles and responsibilities. He attempted to make a connection between myself and the apostle as two women working in corporate America; emphasizing that she knew how to get and manage money.

There was another Sunday service where he was preaching and, in the middle of his message, he made a statement similar to this: "Just because you don't see me post about a relationship doesn't mean that I am not in one. I keep my relationships private."

After that message, he came to me and asked me if I heard how, he stated he was in a relationship. That it was made to let the people know that he was not single. To emphasize that his lack of posting didn't mean that he wasn't taken.

I told him it wasn't like he stated who he was in a relationship with, so that declaration was very vague. He advised me that, in due time, he would let it be known. He stated that you date in secret, court privately, but you marry publicly. That way you never let the right hand know what the left hand is doing. He further stated, in the past, the women he was with experienced an intense amount of warfare if they went public too soon with their relationship; he wanted to protect me from that until we were married. For me, I accepted everything he stated as his reasoning because this was one relationship that was not going to fail.

The Secret Wives

5

DEEP COVER

In October of 2016, he decided to have a "Back to Holiness" revival, in South Jersey. He chose an area the older woman stated she was from and could have a large following to support the services. However, no one showed up for entire three days. Two major preachers showed up, but the people were not there.

One of the guest preachers had prophesied to him about a relationship he was in with a young woman and said I cannot tell you not to do it, but she is not the one. At that time, he and I were dating/courting; I knew he wasn't referring to me because I wasn't a young woman. However, I can remember looking at the young lady when the Man of God said that, and her eyes were wide and shocked. Later that night he had accepted an assignment to preach in Newark, NJ, and we all drove in my car to Newark. Yet, the young lady wanted him to ride with her alone.

When he stated to me that he needed to ride with her, so that she wouldn't be riding alone, I looked at his armor bearer and musician and asked why wouldn't one of them ride with her? I stated emphatically that he was NOT riding in the car with her. If she wanted to come to Newark, and she couldn't drive alone, then she would need to get in the back with them. And that is what she did. For the entire ride to and from Newark, he acted as if he was asleep. When we arrived back to South Jersey, the young woman still had to drive home, and we all had to drive to the hotel we stayed at in South Jersey.

After an extremely unsuccessful "Back to Holiness" revival, the scandals began. You see, the apostle who had released the word about the young woman he was dating not being the one had been paid with a bad check. It bounced when he tried to deposit it. He assumed the older woman was going to cover the payment as she had done in the past. However, this time she was not doing so.

There was a time where he had to preach at a church service in Queens, NY. I attended the service, along with his armor bearer and musician. It was a revival service that lasted for about three days. One night during the revival, I couldn't get back into my aunt's house because the chain was placed on the door. I ended up having to go with him, the armor bearer and the musician to his parents' house. He and I stayed in the bedroom in the basement while the armor bearer and musician slept in family room area. The next morning, I met his parents, and they were very kind to me. I ended up staying there with him for the weekend until the revival was over.

The incidents that occurred prior to the 1st Annual Holy Convocation were monumental! He attempted to accuse the older woman of stealing the church's money, by stating she had opened a church account with PNC Bank unbeknownst to him; and she was the one who wrote the bad check. The young apostle basically advised that he needed to make good on his commitment and pay him his money.

It was at that time he advised me that the church bank account was closed, and the older woman stole the church's money, which was why the payment to the apostle had bounced during the Back to Holiness revival.

Immediately following, another incident occurred via email, where the older woman sent an email to everyone who was supposed to be a guest at the 1st Annual Holy Convocation, insinuating that he was married to a woman in Rhode Island while attempting to carry on a relationship with me, and how he would drive my car to the "wife's" house in Rhode Island and how desperate I must have been to be dating a man and allow him to drive my car to his "wife's" house.

All chaos was breaking loose. We all received the emails at the same time, and he immediately contacted his armor bearer and advised him to handle it.

With that, her and I began a war of words. He vehemently denied being married to anyone, and stated he had proof of his divorce from his first and second wives. He claimed that she (the apostle) was upset that he didn't accept her advances so now she was attempting to ruin his ministry and his name.

The guests who were cc'd on the email where the accusation occurred began to contact the armor bearer to verify what was going on. The armor bearer had to reassure the guest preachers that everything mentioned in the email was a lie and was coming from someone who was asked to leave the ministry.

Believing every word he stated, I defended him wholeheartedly. I defended his character and even called her a witch. She threatened to sue him for every dime she had spent towards the church and his affairs. She began to list everything she had paid for, from flights and hotels to church rent. You name it, she had paid for it. She planned to sue him because he was a fraud.

In my mind, she was just someone whom he denied her advances because, as he stated, she just wanted a young man, and someone who was in a position of power.

After that situation occurred, it left a lot in question for me. As hard as I defended him, I also started to question the validity of his words.

Shortly after the Back to Holiness debacle, he was asked to preach at the church in Queens, NY again. He held service in Asbury Park, NJ and his best friend from childhood preached the regular service. After service was over, we all headed to Queens, NY; the musician rode in the car with his best friend. After that, things began to change.

This is how the woman apostle and his musician learned the truth about him. His best friend was tired of the façade and what was happening in the church. He had began to tell of the true story of the second "wife" and what really happened in Rhode Island. This was the best friend's way of attempting to warn everyone of what was going on in order to stop the bleeding that was happening within the church from a "bishop" who was no more than a mere man, not ready for such a charge.

One evening, his musician called me, and he told me that he needed to tell me the truth. And the musician told me that when he would drive my car to Rhode Island, that he was in fact going to see his "wife" in Rhode Island. He also advised that when they were in California in August of 2016, that he was purposely ignoring my phone calls, and how the musician thought I was such a good woman and didn't deserve what was going on. In his words, he "isn't right."

The musician stated he didn't know he was still married, how he had even lied to him, but his best friend had told him all about it during the car ride to the service in Queens, NY. The best friend felt guilty about everything that was going on and didn't want any parts of the mess he was creating.

So, I contacted him, and asked him to be honest and straight up, to tell me the truth. He stated everyone was coming against him, and he couldn't understand how someone he took in as a son, someone he had helped financially, could come against him. How someone he had taken under his wing to teach him how to become a better musician could turn against him. How everyone he had ever trusted and was close with had turned on him. He explained that when he "divorced" his second "wife" that they didn't announce it, which is the reason why his best friend wasn't aware that they were "divorced." He explained that the "divorce" was very painful for him and how it was very hard for him to talk about it because it caused him to be in a dark place for months. He was finally out of the dark place, and everyone was attacking him.

He even went as far as to have his armor bearer call me on a three-way call with his best friend, and the armor bearer was having an exchange of words with his best friend. The best friend stated to the armor bearer, "So, he's "divorced"?"

The armor bearer replied, "Yes."

The best friend said, "Since when?"

He replied, "Since around January or February of 2016."

When the best friend was about to reply, I was disconnected from the call.

With his detailed explanation and the armor bearer stating the same, I believed him. I thought he was being truthful and sharing his heart. However, the scandals continued.

Afterwards, he had called me but I wasn't available, so the phone went to voicemail. However, he never hung up the phone, and I could hear him speaking to someone. I could not make out the voice, but I could hear them conversing and purchasing Black and Mild's and he was telling her that the musician was done and getting cut-off.

When I questioned him about the voicemail because they were at a Wawa, he told me he was home at his parents' house in Long Island. He added that he had taken a drive, and ran in to his friend who lived in Queens at the store, and he was speaking to that friend.

Since I could hear clearly the purchase was taking place at a Wawa, I knew at that moment he was not telling the truth. However, I didn't press the issue. I didn't have concrete proof that he was lying; and I didn't want to be someone who accused him unjustly.

Afterwards, we began to prepare for Convocation 2016, the 1st Convocation. I noticed that I began to place his needs above my own, never acknowledging the signs that were in front of me. I ignored every one of them and continued in a relationship that was toxic. I lost myself trying to love someone who was incapable of loving himself, let alone loving me.

It almost came to light during Convocation 2016, the first ever Convocation, which is a three-day church convention. His "ex-wife" came from Rhode Island. When she and I first met, she didn't say many words to me. I made a comment to him, saying that she wasn't friendly. However, on the first night of the church service, she was responsible for monitoring the table where the t-shirts and registration were being handled. I sat with her for most of the evening so that she wouldn't be alone. We spoke and had general conversation.

At one point prior to the service beginning, she had gotten up to walk. She tripped and fell, and the other young lady kind of smirked. He made her go to the altar to pray. And he made a comment to me along the lines of: "I'm not tolerating any witchcraft. Make sure she prays until whatever is in her comes out."

I had no idea what was going on with the two women as I was very new to the situation and the equation. However, when the young woman was finished praying, I had her open the service with me in prayer. I wasn't sure what was bothering her, but I could tell she had something on her heart. I had her get up from the altar and I told her to forget whatever it was that she was feeling and focus on the service. And that young woman prayed!

We opened the service up in prayer, as we had done numerous times. It wasn't until the second night of the event when the real drama began to unfold. After the guest preacher finished speaking, I was responsible for counting the offering that night. The guest preacher had stated publicly that he didn't want his honorarium and to ensure everything went to the church. When I went to the back room to count the offering, I noticed his "ex-wife" was in the room and she seemed upset. I inquired with her if she was okay, as I was genuinely concerned. That was when she began to tell me a story about how, when she was in Rhode Island, her friends had prayed for her, and she had a vision that there were three witches at the church in New Jersey that were trying to come against her and keep her and him apart.

At that point I backed up from her. With all the common sense that I did have, I realized the woman had called me a witch, indirectly. When I backed up, and sat in the seat across from her, I told her that I highly doubted anyone was attempting to come in-between her and him. I even told her with as close as she was to him, and her starting up the Rhode Island church again, she would have an integral part of the ministry. Truth is, to me she was his "ex-wife" who was coming because she wanted to restart her ministry. We then laughed about some things pertaining to him, and how he didn't take care of anything that you purchased for him. She told me a story about how he had a coat that she purchased for him tossed in his trunk.

After I completed counting the money, she informed me that she and him were, in fact, married. In that moment, I immediately apologized to her, and told her that he and I were "dating." However, we had never had sex; only kissed and laid in the bed next to each other. I told her that was what I did not do in church and that I was leaving.

No longer than two seconds after she dropped that bombshell, he walked in the back room to inquire about the money. I gave him the money and told him he could count it and I was leaving. He asked why was I leaving, but I didn't stick around to provide him with an answer. I walked out the door.

As I was on my way out of the church, I slammed every door that came my way. Once outside and in my car, he walked out the side door with the guest preacher and some other people. I gave him two middle fingers! I didn't care who was around at that point. To me, that entire Convocation was a shit-show! It was then she came to my car and begged me not to leave, stating that he was going to be upset with her if I left. She stated that she wouldn't have a way home, and I told her she would have a way home because she could leave with me.

One of the guest musicians came to my car to offer his apologies and check to see if I was okay; he had seen what was going on. I told him that I was okay, but I couldn't speak at the moment. The other guest musicians came over to check on me as well. I told everyone that I was fine.

The "wife" came back to my car and asked that I come inside the church; he wanted to have a meeting. I finally obliged to go sit down with them. Once in the meeting, I should have known to record them; there weren't anything but lies being told from the beginning. He opened the meeting by accusing me of asking her if he was married to her. He attempted to engage in a long monologue that I wasn't even trying to hear.

I cut him off and advised everyone sitting in that room that I NEVER asked her if they were married. I detailed what happened in the room.

When I was done, he looked at her and said, "Oh, so we are married now?"

When confronted, she didn't stick to what she had said, and lied. I'm a very direct person; I don't fish for information. I found out there was another woman he was in a relationship with, and it was the young lady who was also a member of the church; the same young lady who I first saw at the service in the Bronx, NY.

I left the church and I'll never forget the pain and hurt I felt. I do not believe in making a mockery of God in the house of God. I would rather not attend church than to sit and be in sin in the church. One thing that I held true to was the fact that he and I had never slept together and barely even kissed. He never pushed me, and I thought that signified his integrity as a man of God.

But the truth was, the young lady had told the guest choir director at the Convocation that they were sleeping together and had been sleeping together; and how they had spent the holidays together. That was completely contradictory to what he told me in the beginning; that he never dated her. The story changed during Convocation when he finally admitted that they went on one date and he realized that she was too young and too immature and looking for a father figure due to her upbringing and wanted someone to raise and be a father figure to her son. He had a "wife," the young lady, me, and other women, one woman who would send him naked pictures. He apologized for it all, and I believed him again.

By the time Convocation 2016 came, the two other women who were members of the church had already left the church. I thought I knew why the apostle left the church. However, I didn't know why the other woman left the church. It was only the young lady and I left in the church.

When he apologized for everything, I wasn't sure if I was going to stay at Convocation 2016. I had a lot of thoughts running through my mind; and one of the thoughts was this was all an entire mess. I had invited my friend to come down from Middletown, NY and he was there witnessing the mess in the church. In speaking with the choir director, she asked me what was it that I wanted to do. If I wanted to leave, she was leaving with me.

I literally packed up my car with everything I had, and I was going to leave in the middle of the night. I reached out to him and told him that I was leaving and never wanted to see him again. He contacted me immediately and told me that he was supposed to be on consecration because the next day was "official day"—the day of licensing for those within the fellowship. However, he felt it was urgent for him to speak with me. He advised me that if I wanted to leave, he would not stop me, but that I should consider how many times I had ran when things had gotten hard, how the next day was official day, and how I had worked hard in ministry for years without being recognized or licensed but had been doing the work.

He advised that I should go into prayer and consult with God regarding what I should do and not act based on my emotions because I had been running for too long.

After we got off the phone, I sat in the car and I waited and I cried, and I waited, and I cried some more. I cried because, in my heart, I really wanted to leave. Yet, in my mind, I was thinking about how many times I had been promised so much in ministry and couldn't seem to get ahead. I thought of how many times I had started the process and not completed it. I thought I was tired of starting and stopping and not completing things through to the end.

It was in that moment that a song came on the radio that spoke to finishing until the end, no matter what it looked like. To me, that was a sign from God that I needed to go back upstairs, get some rest, and finish what I started. That was what I did.

The next day during official day, it was the "ex-wife," the young lady, and me who were all getting licensed. The "ex-wife" was being elevated to pastor, the young lady and I were being licensed as ministers. As we were getting prepared for the service, he gave us a "pep-talk" in the back, advising us that day wasn't about personal emotions but fulfilling the call of God.

However, once inside the sanctuary, the air was thick and off. There was so much tension, hurt, and confusion in the air. They were trying to do praise and worship, but it couldn't go on. The spirit in the room was not right; hurt and pain was felt throughout the sanctuary.

So, I leaned over to the "ex-wife" and the young lady and I said to them the spirit wasn't right in the room and it was due to us. If we were going to do it, we needed to break what was in the room. The three of us got together and began to worship and praise God together.

When we did that, the service went on as planned; however, things still were not right. Imagine, a "bishop" having his "wife," "mistress #1," and "mistress #2" in one church service to get licensed. Then I later found out there was another minister who was visiting to support the 1st Annual Convocation whom he was speaking to romantically too. I also learned after the fact that his first wife had even asked him what he was thinking, having all of us that he was "dating" at the same service to be licensed in church. Understand everything that was going on was in direct violation to the Word of God, to the Spirit of God, to the Character of God, and to the Love of God.

After Convocation was over, he told me I exposed him and left him uncovered, and because of that, I made him angry. I found myself apologizing to him as if I did him wrong. I felt guilty because he expressed to me that was what women had always done to him in the past; left him exposed and didn't provide him a safe place or a covering.

I apologized to him profusely. I never wanted to be someone who hurt him or left him exposed and uncovered. I wanted to provide him with place of safety and comfort; and be someone he could count on. So, for Christmas, I bought him a MacBook Pro to make up for the "exposure." I also purchased his daughter clothes from the Gap and the Children's Place; I had them shipped to his parents' house. It was a bunch of nice dresses, shirts, jeans, everything. I later found out that she never received those items that I purchased. In my mind, I think he took all of those clothes back to the stores, advised them to give him a store credit as opposed to putting the money back on the card and he possibly purchased clothes for the young lady's son as opposed to providing those clothes to his own daughter. Meanwhile, he bought me some fake perfume from Jamaica Avenue in Queens, NY.

I had given him a Pandora bracelet to give his mother. I found it strange that, after seeing his mother on various occasions, she never thanked me for the bracelet. I would ask him did she like the bracelet because I never received a thank you from her. He would say that she told him to tell me thank you, and that she loved the bracelet and couldn't wait for him to purchase her charms for it. However, I never saw her with the bracelet.

Later, I learned he had given that bracelet to the young lady he was dating in the church. A friend of mine was following her on Instagram and she sent me a screenshot of the Pandora bag and bracelet I had given to him to give to his mother.

When I asked him about it, he lied of course and said he never gave her anything, and that she wasn't referring to him in the picture because she was dating a young apostle from Delaware. I believed him but always kept that in the back of my mind.

In December 2016, he was in an accident in my car in Ohio. My car was totaled, the frame was bent, and due to his license issues, he never reported the accident. I paid out of my pocket over $2,000 in an attempt to fix my car. I didn't have a car for almost a month. I was renting cars and paying for them out of pocket with no assistance from him. I remember while he was in Ohio attempting to get my car fixed enough to get it back to New Jersey, I had a friend of mine pick him up from a hotel. My friend advised me there was a woman with him. I asked him about it, and he told me his sister had come up to the hotel. When my friend asked me about it again, I confirmed the woman as his sister. My friend went on to tell me that he kept referring to me as his assistant. Assistant?

Two years later I found out that woman wasn't his sister, but the "ex-wife" from Rhode Island. I was believing his lies because I didn't want to fail. Failure was not an option this time!

Towards the end of January 2017, I was able to purchase a brand-new car from a dealership; a white Chevrolet Malibu with less than thirty miles. When I came to church with the car, he announced to the church how God had blessed me with a brand-new car, and I knew God had done it. I was in the process of rebuilding my credit, and I was able to get that car with no money down, and a low interest rate.

He and I were not in a good place in our relationship, and by the end of January 2017, I had asked him for the laptop and iPad back that I had purchased for him; and told him I was leaving the church and him. We had hit an extremely dark place in our relationship, to the point where he was very disrespectful and had threatened me. I had blocked him from every outlet of contact.

One Sunday morning at five a.m., he reached out to me via FB messenger. He started pouring his heart out to me. He said he loved me, how he needed me, how I couldn't leave him, how he realized how much I meant to him, and that he could see it now. He said I didn't have to come back to the church right away, but for me to go to his spiritual father's church in Jamaica, NY. He said he would tell him that I was coming, and I did.

I sat in the back of the church and received from the Lord what it was that I needed in that moment. I would never forget because after that service, I went to see my cousin. I hadn't seen her in a while. As I sat with her, we were watching the Super Bowl or something on TV. She told me she had breast cancer as she curled my hair, and she and I talked and talked. I had just lost my aunt to ovarian cancer, and that night when I went back to church because his spiritual father had an impromptu second service, I prayed for my cousin, I prayed for me, and I prayed for him. Then his spiritual father did another service. I think it was the next night or the following Tuesday night, and I went then too. He gave out these tissues, blue and red. One to place on your finances, the other to place on your body for sickness.

I had opened the church bank account at Chase bank, in my name and his name. He told me that he had done that because of the level of trust that he had in me and in us. So, I placed the tissue on the church checkbook because it was in a binder and I prayed with the other tissue because he had gone through a cancer scare, where he needed to have surgery on his hand to remove the cancerous mass that had grown.

He wouldn't allow me to be there for the surgery. He called me via FaceTime when he came out of the surgery, telling me that his mother was there with him and his armor bearer. Till this day, I'm sure that was a lie. I prayed and following going to the service at his spiritual father's church, I went back to him. I thought that he had finally awakened to the truth, but that was far from true.

6

THE SECRET WIFE

In April 2017, we moved in together in South Jersey and it was rocky from the beginning. I thought we just needed time to adjust. The truth was when you live with someone, you see it all. I thought I was doing something great by securing our own apartment. Some warned me on several occasions not to be with him while others told me he was my husband. Everyone had very conflicting ideas about him and me.

He was always in and out of the house and would get angry when asked where he was going. He would tell me he was going to visit his parents, which puzzled me. We lived in South Jersey and his parents lived on Long Island, NY. That's a minimum two-hour drive; three hours maximum. So, I would question why was the trip taking him six hours?

One night I received a call that he'd been arrested for driving on a suspended license. However, the information I was receiving from his armor bearer who called me wasn't sitting well within me. I Googled arrest records and found out he was driving in Rhode Island. He was pulled over while on 95-N. I sent the "ex-wife" a message via Facebook Messenger and stated, "I'm aware he was arrested in Rhode Island after he left from home; so please let me know if he needs anything."

The truth was he was nowhere near Long Island. I was irritated with him. Within no more than twenty minutes after that message was sent, he called me to let me know that he had been released and was on his way in an Uber to another location to go to court; and that he would keep me posted on what was going on. I advised him I messaged his "ex-wife" because I figured she would have the information needed. He appeared to be upset and asked why I messaged her because he didn't want everyone knowing his business.

I told him because since he had no family in Rhode Island, who else would he have been seeing in Rhode Island? He kept with his original story of how he was not in Rhode Island, that he was arrested in Queens, NY while on his way to his parents' house; and that when they arrested him in NY, they sent him to Rhode Island because he had outstanding warrants in Rhode Island. I advised him I researched it and could see clearly that he was arrested on 95-N and that was when he advised me that in his family, they didn't like nosey people, and that the report was incorrect.

Later that evening, he contacted me and asked that I drive up the following morning to pick up him. He then provided me with an address and advised that was his cousin's house. He asked that I pick him up early in the morning. He wanted to hurry up and get out of Rhode Island because he was becoming depressed. He stated he had some things in storage in

Rhode Island that he wanted to bring back home, which was his guitar and midi-board. When I pulled up to the building across the street from a funeral home that he stated was his cousin's house, he got in the car and we drove back to New Jersey from Rhode Island.

We lived together from April 2017 – April 2018.

There was a trip made to Ohio in June 2017 while we were living together. I later found out he took that trip with the young woman from the church, and we were living together.

We were at a church service in Wilmington, DE, which was on Pentecost Sunday. The young woman had driven him down to Delaware for that service. Earlier that day, he was preaching in Brooklyn and I ran the service at the church in Newark. Then I drove to Delaware. He was extremely late to the service; but wanted me to get there so that the pastor of the church would know that he was on his way. When they finally arrived at the church, she had an attitude the minute she saw me, and she did not speak.

So, I made a comment, and after the service, an elder from the church came up to me and said, "Are you going to Ohio with them also?"

I thought that was weird. I told her that I wasn't going. I said something to him about it because I wanted to understand why that woman would think that him, the armor bearer and the young woman were going to Ohio. He played the fool and acted as if he wasn't sure.

When we went to the back room after he finished preaching, he gave me a kiss on the lips, told me how beautiful I looked, and for me to get home safe. He was about to get on the road to Ohio and his friend was coming to the church to get them. The young girl and I ended up exchanging words in the back room after the service was over; her attitude was very immature. When he walked me to my car that night, he and I spoke very candidly, so I thought. He ended up texting me later on that night and advised me that the pastor of the church we were at ended up telling the young lady a few things concerning who she was and was not.

However, I think that entire ordeal was a lie and used in a way to manipulate and control me.

Supposedly, I found out later, that she was pregnant and went with him to Ohio for his daughter's graduation. Then, two months later, he and I were in Ohio together for his daughter's birthday party. He lied when he told me he was going to Ohio with a friend of his.

There were countless stories of him dealing with multiple women and disappearing for days at a time. The summer of 2017 was the hardest period of my life and it almost broke me down and tore us apart. In the end, I thought we had made it through everything. I thought we had successfully endured everything that was sentt out to destroy us. We took a trip to meet my father and sister. He had already met my mother and grandmother on another occasion.

During the visit, he asked my father if it would be okay if he married me. My father gave me him his blessing but was sure to tell me, "Kiya, I don't know him. He seems okay, but the jury is still out on him. But if that's what you want to do, then let me know when and I will be there."

We set a date in August 2017, but he ended up in the hospital after a night out. At that point, I was over the entire relationship. He called me from the ER; I went and just looked at him. I was disgusted because deep down inside I knew why he was there, but I was also concerned because something was wrong.

They admitted him into the hospital, and once he was comfortable in his room, I went home to get some things for him. I had expressed to him that I didn't want him at that hospital. I wanted him to sign out to go to another hospital, but he stayed. They finally discharged him and he came home, but the following morning he was worse and we went to Cooper Hospital in Camden, NJ.

It was there that I met two people who ministered to me. He had told them that we were in a relationship but withheld the fact that we lived together. The woman questioned me on marriage, my parents' relationship, and a bunch of other things. She ministered to me concerning him, and it was at that point that I began to cry; not because what she was saying was true, but because she too couldn't see beyond the façade. She told me how broken he was, how hurt he was, how to love him, and how he shouldn't be stressed, but she told him that I was his wife and blessed us to get married. When they left and the hospital discharged him, he looked at me and apologized and said he knew why he was in there, and I said I do too. I told him he had a decision to make because I was tired.

You see, prior to this point, he had married a young couple at the church. When he married the young couple, the day of the wedding he advised me that the young woman would be there because the wife had asked her to attend in order to do her hair for the wedding. I didn't think anything of it. I was never an insecure woman, and because of that I never really questioned the young woman's presence.

What ended up happening was, after the ceremony was over, and everyone left, he and I stayed behind at the church. We then walked down to the store together. When we left the store, I grabbed his hand, but he pulled away from me, claiming it was too hot to be holding hands. At that point, I looked across the street and saw the young woman standing outside with a bewildered look on her face. I kept walking and went to the car. She proceeded to call him on his phone, and he advised that he needed to go speak with her because she was having an issue. As I was sitting in the car, I was speaking with my friend on the phone. After a long while I realized he was still in the church. So, I turned the car off, and decided to see what was going on. When I approached the church doors, I realized the doors were locked. Which at this point, I'm telling my friend that's weird because why would he lock the church doors?

I began to call him and bang on the door. At that point I now needed to use the bathroom. When the door finally opened, the young woman was walking out the door in a haste and didn't even look my way. She appeared out-of-sorts and hurt.

When I left the bathroom, I found him sitting in a room outside of the kitchen in the church; I asked him what happened between her and him. He proceeded to tell me that she put his hands on him and he had to restrain her and that he hit her. I immediately asked him why would they ever argue like that inside of a church to the point where she would put her hands on him and vice versa? I also once again asked him for the nature of their relationship; it appeared what just happened was a lover's quarrel. He advised once again that they had dated in the past, but she couldn't let it go and understand that he had moved on. At that point, as I stated, I am not an insecure woman, so for me that was something for him to handle and not something for me to get involved in.

We decided to move forward with getting married. We went to NY to get his birth certificate. The date we wanted to get married was near, so we had to go to the court to waive the waiting period, and that was granted.

A friend of his who became a very good friend of mine came down to our house one morning. I didn't tell her what for. We went to the vital statistics office in Willingboro, NJ and that was where I told her that we needed her as a witness for us to get our marriage license. And even then, she asked me if I was sure that was what I wanted to do. She had been a witness to some things, things that I didn't even know about until after the fact, but she wanted to be sure that I was sure. I reassured her that he and I had spoken about everything (so I thought) and we were starting with a clean slate, so we got the license.

Every time we set a date for the wedding, there was an issue! He stated as a bishop only an apostle could marry him, so he was going to ask his other spiritual father to marry us. He told me that his spiritual father wanted to meet with us prior to marrying us, but there were issues with scheduling the sessions. Then I asked him if my spiritual father could marry us. He said yes, so I gave him my spiritual father's information, but my spiritual father till this day says that he never contacted him.

We were delayed, and the marriage license was expiring as of 09/30/2017. We finally set the date to get married on 09/29/2017 and we were supposed to be married at the church we were renting from, on that date. Allegedly, the young woman he was previously dating found out we were getting married, and she had planned to come ruin our wedding. Right before we were set to get married, he began asking me a lot of questions, so I told him to cancel the entire wedding. My friend, whom I consider more like my brother, agreed to marry us because he believed in us. I called my brother and told him the wedding was off. I refused to marry in confusion. I was serious about the cancellation, so my brother called him to see what was going on. My brother then called me back and told me to calm down, the wedding was on, and that they (his wife and him) were on their way to our house.

I asked him if he was sure because the license was expiring in one day and we could surely cancel the wedding and go our separate ways. He advised me to go get ready because the wedding was happening, and we were getting married because he loved me.

On September 29, 2017 we got married in secret! He made it clear not to post anything on social media, that we would announce it to the church first, then we would announce our marriage publicly. So, we announced it to the church first and had full support of our church family. We moved in ministry as one but that didn't stop the issues. Publicly we looked great, privately was a different story. As a wife, you never discuss what's going on at home with anyone. I didn't tell anyone about our marital problems with the exception of one friend I trusted.

No one understood the battles we were fighting. When he announced that I was his wife at Convocation 2017, it caused an uproar; according to him he lost ministry assignments and friends. What I wasn't aware of was the person who made him a "bishop" was at our Convocation of 2017; and what he told me after-the-fact was that as he was announcing our wedding and that we were married; someone was live on Facebook and the "ex-wife" heard him announce that we were married. She immediately began to text the Bishop and state that they were in-fact still married, so how could he have married me. However, the Bishop knowing this information never stopped the Convocation, never even stopped him. What he told me was he said to him to just make sure that he didn't make his name look bad. All they cared about was their names; forget the souls of the people who were getting caught in the whirlwind of deception, manipulation and lies as long as his name wasn't tarnished.

After the Convocation, I saw a Facebook post his "ex-wife" had written where she laid her heart out and basically stated they were in-fact still married and how she would, in that moment, begin the divorce proceedings. It was at that time that I asked him if our marriage was legit. He told me our marriage was legit and why would I ask such a question? He said that when he awakened that he felt such warfare; and that is when I showed him the post. I'm not sure if he texted her or called her or something; but I know that post was gone in sixty seconds.

Even with all of that, I felt that he began to resent me. We'd argue a lot. If I posted a picture of him and me on social media, he'd yell at me, telling me to take the picture down. Prior to us getting married, he told me that we had a clean slate. He wanted to clear the air with me and tell me the truth. We went to IHOP on Springfield Avenue in Irvington, NJ. He told me how he and the young woman were in a relationship. At one point, he even considered marrying her. He had met her entire family and yes, she had even gotten pregnant by him but lost the baby. He said that over time he realized that she was not meant to be with him due to certain issues, but that she stayed with the ministry because she said that God told her to be a part of the ministry even though they were not together. He said that she couldn't stand to see him with me, so she left the ministry because she was in love with him, and he had moved on.

The Secret Wives

7

IS IT ADULTERY?

In February of 2018, I had preached on obedience at a service in Allentown, PA. It was after that service that he decided to come clean about his cheating on me twice, once with the young woman, and then another time with another woman from Elkton, MD who was pregnant.

When he told me this woman in Elkton, MD was pregnant, I was crushed. I had gone through two procedures and a major surgery to attempt to conceive. For years, I was told that I would never conceive a child, so to hear that my "husband" had another woman pregnant, I was hurt beyond words. To think that a couple of weeks prior to that, we celebrated Valentine's Day, and he had posted a post on Facebook that my friends took offense to, and they called me. I asked him to take the post down and he did but posted another post that was yet still offensive as his "wife."

On February 15, 2018, I posted a collage of pics with him and me, and almost immediately I was told to take the post down because he was being attacked. I was so hurt that I took the post down and every post that I could find with any mention of him. I can remember sitting on the couch and crying because I was crumbling. We argued that morning and he left for work.

I messaged my sister in Germany and told her I didn't want to live anymore. At that point I'd had ENOUGH! I fell apart. He was abusive, and it was the worst type of mental, emotional, and spiritual abuse that I had ever faced. I had never felt so rejected, so unloved, under-appreciated and taken for granted in all of my years. To have a man, who was supposed to love, protect, provide, and proclaim me, treat me as if I was absolutely nothing; I attempted suicide. I thank God it didn't work; I didn't want to feel anymore. The hurt and the pain had become unbearable. I had to constantly live in secret. I was constantly told that I needed to understand how he felt about his ministry and about what he wanted. Meanwhile, how I felt was neither regarded nor respected.

I had grown extremely tired of all of the lies, and I was barely able to eat or sleep. I was stressed every day; all the while being the one blamed for everything that was wrong. Even though I knew I was not to blame, I took on the blame and accepted everything he stated. I accepted living in secret with a man I was married to because I wanted to protect and cover him, and not expose him. I accepted the weight of living with someone who was abusive verbally, mentally, emotionally and spiritually. Someone who tried to break me down spiritually, tell me my preaching style needed to be like his; because he didn't need to study or put together a sermon with real points, because he was used by the Holy Spirit and that I needed to stop reading all of the books I had and cross-referencing with bibles to produce a solid word; all the things I was taught, he was attempting to undo. I could barely pray. I had lost my strength. I had lost my fight. I had lost my zeal for life and ministry. I was losing me, and I didn't know how to regain me.

One Sunday, he cancelled service and had me drop him off at the train station in Trenton. He said he was going to ride the train and would be home later. That's not what happened. Often times he would state he was going to see some friends in ministry, and it was the guy's night; however, I'm sure most of it was a lie.

The next morning, he called me. I didn't answer the phone, and then he texted me asking me what I was doing. I told him I was going to the movies because this was the weekend that the film *Black Panther* was released, and he decided to meet me at Cherry Hill Mall in NJ. Prior to going to the movies, as he was sitting across from me at the restaurant, I looked at him and immediately began to cry because I knew he was out cheating. I got up from the table to leave. Once in the car, he made it seem like I was the problem, using my past against me. He said I was pushing him away, that he wasn't cheating; he was with one of his male friends relaxing. Later, he revealed that he was indeed cheating. Still attempting to hold on to a marriage and not fail, I proposed marriage counseling.

One Sunday morning we were on our way to church, and he dropped another bomb on me. He'd gotten a woman pregnant. I was crushed. I dropped him off at the church, drove to a parking lot and cried. It was at that time that I had learned that my cousin was in the hospital and I was supposed to go to Paterson to see about her, and I did. I went to the hospital. I put the face on; anyone who is married to someone in ministry will understand the face.

You act as if everything is great, while on the inside you are truly broken. I remember leaving the hospital with my family, and them asking me about him and the church; and I am the face. I knew what to do and what to say, automatically. I kissed them goodbye, and went back to church, and I can remember sitting there hearing him preach, hearing him sing, watching him do all these things like this man didn't tell me as his "wife" that he has another woman pregnant and cheated on me with the same young woman he had told the members that she had left the church because she wanted him and couldn't have him and he wouldn't have anyone in the church disrespecting his "wife."

This same man was preaching, prophesying, and laying hands on the people. I kept getting up and crying in the back office; I couldn't believe that was me. Even through my pain and anguish, a young woman who attended the church needed to be ministered to, so she came to find me because she needed prayer. I had to put the face back on because I was Pastor Kiya, the First Lady, and no one could know what was going on. Inside I was broken, embarrassed, ashamed, and angry.

Another incident happened in February of 2018. He was asked to preach at a service in Delaware; and I set up the agreement for the service. As his wife, I was speaking to the pastor's assistant to solidify the assignment. Once everything was confirmed, she asked me if I would be at the service and I advised her that I would be there.

The day of the service, I picked him up from work; he had started a job at a Honda dealership in South Jersey.

When I arrived to pick him up, I could tell something was wrong, as he kept trying to convince me to stay home and not to attend the service. I told him I was going to service, which appeared to really upset him. As we drove to the service, he started an argument and told me that I better not get upset if I see certain people at the service because it was in Delaware and he had a following in Delaware.

I knew he was referring to the young lady. I asked him did she reach out to him and tell him she was going to the service, and he advised no but that she knew the church and the people where the service was going to be held. I advised him that church was free for everyone, and that he and I were married so why would I care that she was at a free church service. However, that did not stop the argument from continuing to the point where he attempted to blame me for causing his spirit to be vexed and how I needed to understand how I should not upset him prior to him having to minister at a service. I was so angry, I told him I wasn't going to go in the church.

As I drove to the church, I changed my mind; however, I didn't say anything to him until we pulled up in front of the church. When he got out the car, he advised that he would call me when done, and I snapped and advised him I was parking the car and coming inside.

When I sat in the church, I originally sat in the back of the church because I was highly annoyed. He had called me to ask me to go to the ATM to get money for the offering. When I arrived back to the church, I noticed the young lady was there. I went upstairs to give him the money for the offering, and I went back downstairs and sat in the front of the church on the side.

When the service started, I noticed he had taken his wedding band off. I saw the pastor ask him something to which it appeared he didn't respond to; she introduced him and he took to the podium. And it was there that he made a statement along the lines of people wanting to be seen and acknowledged. As the service progressed, the young lady jumped in to help while he was ministering to the people and I didn't say a word.

There was a situation where he needed help with a person in the church, and I didn't move to assist him. I sat in the pew, and he looked at me and signaled for me to help with the person. I pointed to the young lady and told him to send her. When she saw that, she helped with the person as I was not moving.

After that, when it was time for the people to sow, as they sowed he was laying hands on them and giving them a word. He called the young lady up to him and she kneeled down on one knee as he spoke to her without the microphone to his mouth so that no one could know what he was saying. Then I went to give money for the offering and he attempted to give me an off word and act as if that word came from God, telling me that I was worried about the wrong things. I didn't budge at the sound of that word because I knew it was a word from the flesh and had nothing to do with God.

During the service it began to snow. When the service was over, we were upstairs in the office when the pastor came in the office, and she introduced herself to me officially. She asked him, "This is your wife, right?"

He stated, "Yes, this is my wife."

She attempted to tell him she was asking him during service if he wanted me to introduce him, but he advised her that he couldn't hear her, which was why he did it himself.

She then advised me that she noticed the other young lady there, and that she now could recognize the spirit that was in operation. She told him how she remembered when she first saw them (the young lady and him) together and they were engaged to be married; and how she had a dream and told him the young woman was not his wife. She never had the opportunity to tell him so once she saw me, she felt her dream was confirmed.

However, he attempted to twist the situation on me when I refused to help with the person and told him to send her. I stood my ground with him and told him exactly what I thought of that entire fiasco of a service, from him taking his wedding band off, to her assisting with ministering to the people; down to the off word he provided and what the pastor stated when we were in the office.

Of course, he had an explanation for everything! Once we arrived home, he dropped me off and stated he would be right back because his armor bearer had called him and was stuck in South Jersey and needed to speak with him. He was supposed to be bringing home food, and the snow was coming down pretty hard. I had gotten hungry, and he wasn't answering his phone or responding to text messages.

So, I walked in the snow to the 7-Eleven, out of pure frustration and anger. When I arrived back home, he still wasn't there. I decided I would deal with him when he arrived. Upon his arrival, he realized I had gone to the store and asked how did I get to and from the store, and I told him I walked in the snow. It was a pretty bad snowstorm that day; however, due to how angry I was, I didn't even realize it. Until this day, I have no idea who he was with that night, but I know it wasn't his armor bearer; he came back with half-eaten food from Taste of Soul Restaurant in Burlington, NJ.

It was downhill from there, FAST! We argued almost daily. We entered marriage counseling where I expressed what our issues were. I felt they were focusing on the fact that he was a bishop and not the fact that he was an adulterous man, cheating on his wife.

Nikiya Mone

8

THE TRAUMA

In March of 2018, while he was on a ministry assignment in California, I learned I was pregnant. The Friday before I learned I was pregnant; he was ministering at a church service in California. Prior to the service, he called me to let me know he was at the church and about to minister. He needed to tell me something. What he proceeded to advise me was the young lady had traveled to California to surprise her friend at the service, and that he saw her at the hotel. He advised me that he was staying at a completely different hotel from where everyone else was located, but in the honor of full disclosure, he wanted to let me know. I told him I was not concerned with it at all; however, I found it odd that she would travel all the way to California for a church service. But nevertheless, there wasn't anything that I could do from NJ. However, when we had our counseling session before he was leaving to California, where I had advised that I had reservations, those reservations were being confirmed.

I was scheduled to have a procedure done on March 12, 2018 and lo and behold I was pregnant; the procedure was canceled. My spiritual mother, Mia, was with me that day. As I was getting dressed to leave, they brought her to the back and she immediately thought something happened. I could hear her voice filled with concern as the nurse was telling her she was bringing her to me.

Through the door, I could hear her asking, "Well, where is she? What happened?"

I peeked my head out of the door and told her I'm right here. She looked confused, and I could tell she was wondering why I was getting dressed. I told her the procedure was canceled because I was pregnant. She immediately dropped everything that was in her hands, screamed and hugged me tightly. The first thing she asked me was did I call my "husband?" I advised her that I did try to call him, however I could only reach his voicemail. It was at that time she told me not to worry about him, and to focus on me and the baby that I was carrying. She told me to not allow whatever it was that he was doing to bother me because the baby would feel every emotion. She and I left the doctor's office and we drove so that I could get some food; prior to the procedure, I couldn't eat. When he finally called back hours later and I shared the news. However with the young lady mysteriously "showing up" in California and magically appeared at the church service he was also attending and suddenly he was unavailable; things were looking very suspicious and I questioned the people he was in California with. How many of them knew that this married man was seeing another woman?

What I later learned from a "prophet" who was there in California was that when he showed up with the young lady, he was asked what happened to me. He advised his person that he and I were no longer together and he had moved on and was engaged to this young lady.

While they were in California, I saw pictures from the church service, and I saw the young lady had his camera in her hand, as if she was taking pictures. That was the camera I had purchased for him for Christmas because we were using it for the church services. When I saw it in her hands, I screenshot the post and questioned him about the camera and if that was in fact his camera. He told me that the camera she was holding wasn't his, as he would NEVER do that; and the camera she was holding was her friend's camera.

There were so many times where he would use the bishops, apostles, pastors in church as scapegoats for his affairs, he would always say he was at their church services. He would use this one Bishop often and say they were in Atlantic City together because the Bishop had a service and wanted him there. He would use this other female Apostle who had a church in south jersey as a scapegoat and say he was going to her services. He would use his friend as a scapegoat and state he was with his friend because his friend was playing the keys for someone and he was riding with them. One time he said this same friend had a gig to play for the Made in America concert in Philadelphia, PA; this was the one where Mary J. Blige was headlining; and that he was going to be used as a stand-by keyboardist; and he claimed they all had to be on the bus to get there; and he was going to see if the friend could get me a ticket.

All of that was a lie, every word he spoke was a lie; and I honestly until this day I look at every last one of those Bishops, Apostles, and pastors differently because they all condoned his mess.

I always felt if they would have dealt with him, then no woman would have had to be subjected to him; however, everyone had always covered for him and excused his behavior. Why? I believe it was because they all had so much dirt on each other that if one came out against the other, then they all would have been exposed. So for them, it was like the blue code of silence for the police. Those bishops, apostles and the like had a church code of silence or an episcopal code of silence. They would hide everything; they would cover everything as long as it kept their sins covered.

Many would ask me why I would believe his lies, and the truth was I didn't want to believe the truth. The truth was the man had no clue on how to love, how to be faithful, how to honor, how to protect, how to uphold, how to cherish; not even how to be thoughtful. He had a story for everything, there was a reason for everything; and I wanted to believe the reasons; until everything was lit up for me to see.

When he returned from California, he advised me that the "prophet" out there gave him a prophetic word and advised him to stay a little longer in California because stress was trying to cause him to have a heart attack. The so-called prophetic word came at the right time, because when he returned from California, he fell asleep on the couch and his phone rang. When the phone rang, it was face up and I could see a picture of the young lady and him together with a nickname as her name. I kindly woke him up and told him that she was calling him and he might want to take that call. Of course, like the robot that he was, he immediately started an argument. I wasn't even attempting to argue because I was pregnant and I was really trying not to stress myself or the baby. It was on this day that I knew our marriage was over.

When he returned was when things really began to be exposed concerning him and the young lady and the real details of the California trip. Every place he stated he went to visit, she was right there and posting pictures. She also posted a picture of them on the flight together, sitting next to each other. There was another picture posted of them outside somewhere, which he stated she captured the picture, and he was just "being nice" and didn't want to make a scene in front of the hotel, so he obliged by taking the picture.

Once again, he attempted to bring up my past failed relationships and tell me yet again that I was making things up in my mind. He was sure, after his trip to California, that he wanted us to be together and raise our baby together.

The first few weeks after learning I was pregnant, I had to go to the doctor's once a week because they were monitoring the baby's heartbeat; they stated it wasn't as strong as it should be for as far along as I was. But after every visit the baby's heartbeat got stronger and stronger. Between the first and second visit to the doctor for my ultrasound, they were still concerned about the baby's heartrate; it was increasing but not strong enough. By the time of the second sonogram, and the heartrate still wasn't as strong, the third sonogram was scheduled. When I arrived home from the doctor, I had audio recorded the baby's heartbeat and sent it to him. He asked that I come over to him, so he could pray over my growing belly. When he laid his hands on my belly, he began to utter words that I couldn't make out. I felt extremely uneasy about what he said, so immediately when he was done, I texted my brother/friend and his wife and I asked them to please pray. I had no idea what he said over my baby, but I wanted it canceled.

The last sonogram I received on April 5, 2018 the heartbeat was so strong they didn't schedule me another appointment until the end of April.

It was that same day that everything changed! I was experiencing all day sickness being eight weeks pregnant; and he had an assignment to release the word of God at a church launching service in Irvington, NJ. I stayed home and he encouraged me to stay home because I was pregnant and experiencing extreme nausea. As I stayed home and honestly sat on the couch, we had a big leather sectional with the recliner seats, and I was laid back, eating crackers and speaking to my father. My father and I were talking about cheating, and my father was saying how the worst thing a man could do to a woman was cheat on her because that destroyed a woman.

Right after speaking with my father, I noticed that one of his friends was trying to reach me via Facebook messenger. She couldn't get through because I was on the phone with my father. She was trying to reach me to let me know that he was taking this young woman to church with him in Irvington. Even though I was sick, I got in my other car and drove to Irvington.

When I pulled up to where the church was located, I drove around until I spotted my white Chevy Malibu. Once I spotted it, I parked my SUV behind it and unlocked the car door (with the spare key). I moved the car around the corner. I then walked back to my SUV and pulled it in to the spot where he had parked the white car.

I walked inside of the church and spotted where he was sitting in the front row and she was sitting down in the pew about 3 rows behind him, holding his hat and sweat towel. I grabbed that sweat towel off her lap; she jumped up and ran to him. He called me over to him, told me not to embarrass him. I told him he should have thought about that before bringing his whore to church. I walked away and sat right back down. I was angry, but I knew church was not the place for my anger. As I got up to leave, at this point his whore decided to throw water on me. I turned around quickly. I was going to grab her up, but the only thing I could grab was her bag and his hat. I wasn't able to get a hold of her. However, as I walked out of the church with her bag, his hat and towel, I threw them in the middle of the street.

I got in my car and pulled up to the front of the church to see them both outside. I jumped out the car and two people walked up to the car to speak to me. I told them I was his "wife" and he was there with his whore. I showed them my license to prove I was his "wife."

They both said, "Ma'am, I'm so sorry, but he needs to leave. This is not allowed in the church."

All I could think was, *this is crazy!* I called my friend and she met up with me, so we could get the other car moved. I parked the car at her house and I drove home. As I drove home, he began sending me threatening messages because he realized the car was gone. While driving I contacted my friend/brother to tell him what was going on; and he and his wife were so deeply angry and concerned for me at the same time because I was in fact, eight weeks pregnant. My brother advised me to go to the police and file a police report against him for him threatening my life; and I promised my brother that I would do just that. As he was threatening me, I went to the Willingboro police department, and pressed charges against him for the threats and requested a restraining order against him.

While I was at the police station, she drove him home. When he got there and realized the car wasn't there, he called the police to say that I stole his car. I had already been to the police station. So the police told him I was there filing charges against him, and he came to the station with her, and his armor bearer. He was served with a temporary restraining order. The officers made me tell them where the car was, so he could be informed. The officers made me give them all of my information because he was telling them that the car was his and that I stole it. When they looked up the information, they saw that both cars were solely in my name and neither car had his name on it. That was when he advised them that for my SUV, he had contributed 1,200.00 towards the down payment. I advised them that he did. They then attempted to tell me that, since we were married, he would be entitled to half and one of the cars, so I needed to tell them where the car was located. I told them that he was a liar and a fraud and that he and his whore would not be getting in my car.

The police officers, who were all men, made the comment of, "Hell hath no fury like a woman scorned," and it was at that moment that I knew they were going to force me to give them the location to the car. So I told them the around about location, and the name of my friend where I left the car at. However, they couldn't find her name in their system to locate her exact address. I only told them she lived by Lyons in a roundabout way.

So, my husband had his whore begin calling and messaging my friend on Facebook to get her address, so he could pick up the car. Not only did they message her, but they also contacted her sister to get the address. Because I knew he had received the address, I immediately after leaving the police department, my sister and I drove up to Irvington, and moved the car again.

After that he began telling people that I was lying, that I wasn't his "wife," and that he and the young woman were engaged and getting married. He told people that I was delusional because I wanted him but he didn't want me so I came to the church service to embarrass him and his fiancé.

Since he was lying, I posted the truth with receipts on Facebook. I had our marriage certificate and I had my driver's license, but he then tried to say my sister is a graphic artist and she fabricated the documents. He was caught in his lies and the truth was exposed.

A week later, I instructed him to move out of our house, and that I was filing for either a divorce or an annulment. I told him we could coparent, but if I found out that he had our baby in the presence of that young woman, he would never see our child again. He came home, took all his clothes and belongings, packed up the car, and left. I called him and told him to bring me the car. I didn't trust that he wasn't with that young woman, and I didn't want her in my car. So, he came, dropped the car off, and left again.

I was working with Rhode Island vital records to determine if he was legally married in that state to the woman he always stated was his "ex-wife." My mother began to help me search for records. And we couldn't find anything about him being married in Rhode Island. We found his marriage and divorce record for his first marriage; but nothing on the second marriage. What I did uncover by locating the marriage and divorce record for his first marriage was that his first marriage didn't legally end until after he married the second "wife." He married the second wife in May, but his divorce was not finalized from his first wife until June (the following month). With that information, I decided to call Rhode Island Vital Records of Providence County, and I explained to them the situation. I advised them a woman repeatedly stated she was married to my husband in Rhode Island, but he denied being married in Rhode Island. I advised them he showed me a divorce card completed and filled out by them for Providence County. It was then that they advised me there was no such thing as a divorce card. I told them he advised that they were Common Law married in Rhode Island and although there was a ceremony, the pastor didn't submit the marriage license in time. He stated they were never in possession of a marriage certificate, but because Rhode Island recognizes Common Law, they were Common Law married. According to him, when you separate from Common Law marriage, they provide you with a divorce card. The woman advised me that entire situation wasn't possible because even Common Law married couples must go through a standard divorce. The woman advised me to send her a copy of our marriage certificate and my driver's license; I did that via overnight mail. And I waited. Originally, due to privacy rules, they declined my request for information; and I truly felt defeated. I called my mother and advised her they would not release the Marriage Certificate to me, that would in fact show that he was married to his second "wife" in Rhode Island. Since I come from a family of strong women, my mother told me not to give up; to call back and request a supervisor, and I did just that. Once I spoke with another woman, she advised me she would call me prior to 3 p.m. that day. She needed to speak with the head registrar to see if she would be able to send the requested information to me on the grounds of bigamy. And I waited. When she returned the phone call, she said advised on the grounds of bigamy, she could release the short form of the marriage certificate. I was ecstatic because I knew that was exactly what I needed to annul the marriage. I had to send them a money order via overnight mail in order to receive the marriage certificate; this process literally took about three days.

On April 24, 2018, I felt something was wrong because I wasn't experiencing the pregnancy symptoms that I'd once had. The frequent urination and nausea stopped along with all the other symptoms. I made an emergency appointment. While on my way to the doctor, I was on the phone with Mia, my spiritual mother. I was telling her I felt something was wrong, and that I couldn't detect the heartbeat using my at-home heartbeat monitor. She attempted to comfort me and tell me everything was going to be okay. At that time, he went live on Facebook, and texted me and told me to watch his live. Since I had two phones, I connected to the live with my other phone and played it so that my spiritual mother could hear it as well. We listened to this man live on Facebook, completely lying and not telling the whole truth. This man was attempting to apologize for all that had transpired earlier in the month at the church service, he attempted to apologize for causing the ones he loved pain and embarrassment. After he ended the live, he called me and advised me that was his public apology for me. I told him then, it couldn't have been for me when he never said my name, and it appeared as if he was in the young woman's car, so I was sure he told her the same lie. I advised him I was at the doctor's office because something was wrong and that I would call him when I was done. After he and I hung up the phone, he didn't know that my spiritual mother was on my other phone and could hear everything he said. She couldn't believe the level of deception he was willing to go to in order to continue to play with my emotions. When I arrived at the doctor's office, I learned that my baby's heart stopped and died. At first, I couldn't believe it, I thought the tech forgot to turn the volume up on the ultrasound machine. For weeks prior I couldn't wait to hear the sound of my baby's heartbeat. I recorded the sound every time I went to the doctor. The same tech just weeks prior who was congratulating me on my baby having a healthy sounding heart, was now apologizing to me for not detecting a heartbeat. I curled up in that chair in the doctor's office and I cried.

For years I was told I was barren and would never conceive. I finally conceived and experienced so much trauma that my baby couldn't survive. I was distraught, and I blamed him for it all. I called him to let him know the baby died. He acted distraught and hurt and told me he would stop by after church.

My spiritual mother met me at the doctor's office, as soon as I called her and told her the baby died. She came right there. I was leaving and she asked me where I was going, and I didn't know. She told me to come to church with her and I went with her. After church, my spiritual father and her told me to stay at their house and rest until the morning. But I didn't want to; I wanted to go home and sleep in my own bed.

As I left their house, I called my sister as I was driving. She and I were speaking as I was driving. I made a detour and decided to stop at our church. I went by the church because I didn't want him in my house. I wanted him to know how I felt while he was at the church as opposed to him coming to my house. So, upon arrival at the church I was met with him being there with this girl.

I wasn't even angry with him. I just looked at him and said, "Really, this is what you are doing in the church?" It wasn't about me or her in that moment; it was about the church.

He asked that we go outside, and I obliged. The girl decided to follow, even after he told her to go back inside the church. She refused and began to refer to him as "her stuff," and I laughed because "her stuff" was married to me and his second "wife." It amused me that this woman was claiming a man who truly could not be claimed. However, I remembered it was me, standing with him and for him; so in that moment I wasn't even upset with her. Something told me to record this scene because I felt it could go left, so I went live on Facebook to expose the truth of what he was really doing.

The truth was, this wasn't the first, second or third time he'd done this. This was his way of life and there needed to be concrete proof. I had lost my baby and this man was truly playing me all along. So, I went off using every cuss word I could muster. Meanwhile, at the same time they are holding church service inside of the church with a guest "bishop;" and there was all hell breaking loose just outside the church doors in Newark, NJ on Bergen Street. You see, the church was no longer in Bloomfield, NJ because once again, he was not paying the church rent; but asking me for the rent money and I was providing it to him. So, beginning on Resurrection Sunday (Easter Sunday) we had moved the church to another building in Newark, NJ, the irony in that was that same church was a church that his grandmother had helped to establish many years ago, and the Bishop and his wife remembered my husband from when he was a little boy and would travel with his grandmother to that church. They also knew that he and I were married, they even knew that I was pregnant. But truth is none of that mattered on April 24, 2018; I was being attacked in front of that church, all the while, there was preaching, praying and prophesying going on within the walls.

What amazed me was the reaction from these so-called leaders in the church. They didn't care that this man was caught cheating on his "wife" with the other woman, or the fact that it was on video and they could clearly see and hear this young lady attack me up until I threw my phone down and began to fight back. Not that they couldn't hear him as he jumped into the fight, and you could hear me telling him to get off of me; and at that point you could hear him hitting me and glass shattering which was from him putting my head through the car window. They only focused on why I was using profanity. They didn't focus on hearing the glass shatter because he put my head through the car window; they didn't focus on the fact that I was carrying a dead baby on the inside of me, while this man attempted to have his "woman" attack me in front of the church on Bergen Street in Newark, NJ. No one cared except to highlight that I was cussing. Much like what is going on today in the church, when famous gospel singers are caught cussing; it's like as if they major in the minors and minor in the majors.

They acted as if they didn't hear him cussing about coming to his church and telling me I better get the fuck out of there. They acted as if they didn't see that the video mysteriously was "deleted" from Facebook, after watching the entire ordeal live. Nope, not that manmade church that covers for their manmade created leaders. They only wanted to focus on me, and cussing.

Even after he put my head through the car window, I immediately went to the police station and pressed charges against him. He attempted to go to the police precinct too and lie. He and the girl decided to come up with a lie that I attacked her; they didn't think there was any proof of the altercation.

When she and I began to fight, I threw my phone to have both hands ready. When I threw my phone, my Facebook live was still going; the sound was connected to my Bluetooth. The viewers could hear everything that was going on, but they couldn't see what was going on. People immediately began to text my sister and other friends who lived in the area of Newark to see if anyone could get down to the church because they could hear him punching me in the face and they could hear the window shattering.

What many didn't know was that my sister was on the phone with me. She was still connected to my Bluetooth and she could hear everything that was going on. She could hear them attacking me; she could hear the glass shattering; she could hear everything that happened.

One friend told me one of her friends was on the live and texted her and told her to get to the church because they were jumping me in front of the church. Another friend sent his wife down to the precinct once they knew I was okay and I was at the precinct on Lyons Avenue in Newark; and his wife came. She sat with me the entire time. She was there when he and the young woman walked in the precinct. She witnessed them attempt to lie to the officers. She watched him attempt to antagonize me with kissing the girl in front of me. She even heard him say to me, "I'm glad that baby died," with him knowing full well that I was still carrying my baby in my womb, lifeless.

My spiritual mother had called me, and I had her on speakerphone and she could hear him lying in the background. Even one of his friends called me, and she sent me the screen recorded video of the live, because she said when she saw what was going on, she knew I would need proof of what they did to me.

He even attempted to act like he didn't know who she was, after he and I had been to her house numerous times, after all he considered her father-in-law to be like a spiritual father to him. Every lie that he ever told was being exposed on April 24, 2018. When the window shattered, I woke up!

Truth is, I was weakened, beat up, and struck down by this church! And I allowed it because I ignored the signs. I lost my strength and my power. I lost who I was because I was so focused on not failing. I was so focused on filling a void. I was broken and looking for love, acceptance, and even validation in a man. I was lied on, speculated about, talked about, blackballed and outcasted by the same church that I felt was supposed to love and protect me, guide me, even correct me and judge me righteously. But in this situation, they all sided with the man with a title, one who wasn't even worthy of the title or the position. One who abused and manipulated; that is who they sided with; meanwhile leaving the woman to fight for herself, to pick herself up, to find her strength after the trauma. I can remember dealing with the domestic violence advocate in the court, attempting to meet with her; she wouldn't return my phone calls. I drove up to the court in Newark, NJ to provide her with every bit of evidence I had against him. She wasn't in and they told me I would have to come back. Once again, I felt that the victim was being victimized by a court system that should have been fighting for me. So, the day we had court, for him to face the charges of domestic abuse, I dropped all of the charges. The prosecutor asked me if I was sure, and I told her yes, I was sure. They weren't going to cause me to keep taking days off of work. She asked me did I fear him, and I told her absolutely not.

After I dropped the charges, he texted me asking me for a kiss. That's how sick, twisted and demented his mind was. After that he would text me every now and then; he was holding a revival in NC, and he would text me prior to him having to preach and ask me for prayer. I remember he actually called one time after he finished preaching and he told me in a certain number of days, God was going to bring us back together. The date would have been around October or November of 2018; that God said he was going to do it. He told me that he released the word at the revival in NC and told me he had to tell me what the Lord spoke. He even said he would bet me $1,000.00 that the word would come to pass. Little did he know I already had what I needed.

9

BIGAMY IN THE CHURCH!

I found out he was indeed, still married to the woman in Rhode Island, and they'd been married since May of 2014. Prior to April 24, 2018 I had received the confirmation and proof I needed the week prior. However, I held the information in a manila envelope in my closet. I got nervous, thinking one day he could enter the apartment and find the proof. I moved the paperwork to my car and hid it under the passenger side seat.

The young couple that he had married the summer prior had come over to my apartment to check on me and see if I was okay. When they arrived, we spoke in detail about everything that transpired thus far regarding me catching him at the church service with the young lady on April 5, 2018. I told them I had suspicion that he was still married to the woman in Rhode Island, and I re-hashed the post she had made when the announcement was made at the 2nd annual convocation. It was then that the husband told me he still had the screenshot of the post; and I asked him for the screenshot; because I told him I was waiting to get proof from Rhode Island. He had advised that he would look through his phone, and that he was sure he had it. However, what he didn't know was that I already had the proof. A couple of days later, I received a text message from my "husband" advising me that he knew I was poking around and asking around for information concerning his marriage and that I would never find any proof of a marriage because there wasn't one. Even then, I never let him know that I had the proof.

When he was arrested on April 24, 2018, he spent about a week in Essex County Jail. He made sure that no one would be able to see his arrest record because he gave the prison the incorrect spelling of his last name, which I found hilarious. So the prison record was under the incorrect spelling, but the police report and arrest record were under the correct spelling. He was in there for about a week due to other warrants that came up. Once he was locked up, I began receiving telephone calls from everyone, from the court, to the police, to even people in the church. He had told this one woman, who was the owner of the car that he shattered her back window with my head, he told her that I had picked up something and busted out her window on purpose. Even after her hearing the truth, she attempted to call what really happened a lie because I wasn't in the hospital seriously injured. That's how sick people can become when under narcissistic control; they can shape your reality and make you believe even what is false as if it is true.

When he was released from the prison, the prison was sending his court dates and all paperwork to my apartment because my apartment was still listed as his place of residence. When the mail kept coming to my house, I called the court because I had a restraining order against him and was not supposed to be in contact with him and I told them they were sending paperwork to my address but needed to find his address. I had texted him the information from the paperwork, and he asked if we could speak in person. I told him I didn't want to meet with him in person, and he advised that he just wanted to speak.

The only way that I could feel comfortable was to speak in a public place away from our home. When we met at a diner, he sat across from me still lying. He advised he wasn't with the young lady, how he was back staying at his parents' house. He even told me he was not married to the woman in Rhode Island. And I looked at him plainly and told him to stop lying, that I already had the proof that he was married and will be filing for our marriage to be annulled. I also advised him although I had an active restraining order against him, he needed to go to the apartment and remove his name off of the lease by signing the "Roommate Release Form." And he did just that, he asked me how the D & C was, because the Friday after the altercation I was scheduled for the D & C to have the baby removed. My spiritual mother and my sister were with me the entire time. I told him everything was fine and he apologized for putting his hands on me. I told him I could not believe he did that to me, and it was then that he attempted to kiss me and told me that he would make everything right and be back home.

You see, one would have to understand that he would not stop with attempting to manipulate me, he would not stop trying to hold on to an emotional connection with me, he would not stop attempting to mind fuck me into believing a false reality. When I say the depth of his manipulation saw no end, I really mean it saw no end!!

When I filed for an annulment on the grounds of bigamy I had to hire a process server in order to serve him. For a month, the entire month of May, he was attempting to evade being served, coming up with all types of lies to not be served with the annulment paperwork. I had to find out when he was having church service and alert the process servers to have him served on a Sunday morning, June 3, 2018. Within weeks I heard that he in fact, married the young lady. This bishop, as of June 2, 2018 (according to what was confirmed by those close to the couple) was legally "married" to three different women in three different states and the church seemed to accept it all.

Going through this entire experience taught me a valuable lesson about myself. I had to learn who I was. Somewhere after the death of my aunt, I lost me. I was no longer strong and standing in my convictions, but I became a walking concession. I compromised my faith, integrity, joy, and peace to be with a man. He was viewed as a man of authority, power, and influence, but was really an imposter and I fell for it. I decided to ignore everything and pray to God that things would get better.

Even after all of that, I wanted to make peace with him. He was arrested for the domestic dispute between him and me. I met up with him at a diner down the street from my house. He apologized to me for everything. I had nothing but tears to offer. I couldn't believe he did all of that to me. I had dropped the restraining order against him in an effort to move on peacefully. I needed to be able to recognize myself in all of this. It was easy to blame him, but the truth was I signed up to live a lie. I wanted to understand why I allowed the abuse on all levels. I needed to know my own worth. Once I realized that I allowed myself to be devalued, because I didn't value myself; and that I deserved to be loved, the healing process began.

When you constantly devalue yourself and you are not living in purpose, you will attract people and situations that don't add any value to you and will hinder the purpose on your life. I had to learn that about the relationships I entertained. I was no longer tolerant of anything that disrupted my peace. I had to learn that I was valuable, that my presence was valuable, and if I offered you the value of my words, then don't take even my conversation for granted.

Even after him, there were two relationships that were attempted, which ended very quickly. And the reason they ended quickly was because those two men were very similar to him; they constantly had their hands out and my value was based on what I could do for them. However, no one saw that my heart was hurt and damaged; and didn't realize what I needed was support, strength, care, genuine friendship and love. What I was finding was the same old spirit manifesting differently; and it was manifesting differently because I was still walking in the healing process and I still had some residue within me to resolve.

As I journeyed through the healing process, I began to learn a lot about myself. I learned a lot of what I absolutely didn't want and what I absolutely wanted and needed. I started to place me first and get to know who I was intimately.

I had moved out of NJ and started my life over again in MD. Once in Maryland, I was able to fully regroup and heal away from the place that hurt me. I had even taken a break from church, and I would only attend services online. I knew I needed a break from everything and everyone; and I honestly think moving to Maryland restored me, revived me, strengthened me, and repositioned me.

I started to look at life differently, and all things started to make sense.

I had already written in my first book, and it was about to be published; at that point, there was no going back.

During that time, I had received multiple phone calls about me telling my story but on a more public level. But I had shied away from doing that. I didn't want everyone to know; those who knew, knew. If you didn't know, you just didn't know. It wasn't until one day, he had taken things a little too far with his recollection of the events that took place, and I had gotten wind of it. I decided it was time to tell the truth.

I reached out to a vlogger who was known for telling these stories and provided him with all of the truth he needed, the video recording, text messages, marriage certificates, everything I had.

He called me and we spoke, he advised he was going to post the video and if the video went viral, he would do the story. And needless to say, the video went viral and the very next day we were preparing to do the story.

I was living in Maryland, and I was finally dating someone I thought would be it. He came over to my house to sit with me as I recounted the story as if it was yesterday. He sat with me as I recounted what happened, what led up to April 24, 2018, and what happened thereafter.

He was also there to read the comments, and read how the same church people who would sing your praises when then yell crucify her at the same time; especially the women. They picked me apart in those comments; and called me everything known to man except a child of God. I found it humorous that so many people had such an opinion on someone else's life. But what I found astonishing was how they attempted to diminish even my womanhood. I can remember a caller calling in to the show and adamantly stated that I was no lady. In my mind, I truly wished that she was in my face uttering those words.

Everyone had the same question: why did she stay after all the signs were clearly there? The one thing no one could understand was why would I ignore the signs and stick around for the grand finale. Truth is it wasn't intentional, it wasn't like I set out to be hurt, it wasn't like I set out to be cheated on, it wasn't like I set out to be manipulated. In my mind, God had shown me this man's heart and his vulnerable side, and it was my job to love him and not leave him like he said everyone else had done. He said everyone left him when they realized he was human. But the truth is they didn't leave once they recognized he was human; they left because he was abusing them and they more than likely couldn't take it any longer.

I can remember a time during one of his "dark moments" as he called it, he threatened to tie me up and torture me to the point of no return and that no one would be able to find me. As opposed to being afraid, I dared him to try to do it.

There was a time when I was going to preach at a service, and he annoyed me so badly right before leaving the house to preach I threw my ring at him; and he told me I was lucky that he was trying to remain calm and do to me what he has done to others. Again, me not being scared, dared him to try me because unlike the others, he didn't scare me. I still had to go preach at a seven last sayings service. I was pregnant at that time.

I dealt with it all because to me, failure was not an option. I didn't want to be the one who regretted making the decision to stay. It wasn't until the window shattered that I realized that I was failing with him; and in order to succeed in life I needed to leave him and never look back.

After I did the interview with the vlogger; there were multiple women who messaged me via Facebook

Messenger to let me know that they were with him around the same time as I was. Both described my white car and knew the exact year, make and model of the car, and told me how he would drive to see them. One of the women lived very close to where we were living in Willingboro, NJ; she stayed around the corner. Another lived in another part of NJ and the other woman lived in NC. The woman in NC told me how he told her I was his admin because he wanted her to come to the convocation, we had in 2017.

When she told me that, I immediately remembered when he told my friend in Ohio that I was his admin as well.

If you remember in the beginning of the story, I told you about a woman apostle who was part of the ministry but had subsequently left; well, she reached out to me too. She reached out to me through a mutual friend. She and I spoke in great detail surrounding what was going on and lo and behold, he and she were actually dating; but according to her she refused to sleep with him. It was his best friend who told her the truth about him; and that was the reason she sent the email out to everyone that was participating in the 1st annual convocation. She and I spoke about her attacking me in that same email; and what I began to understand was the lies he was telling others about me that caused them to look at me differently. What became clear was he told half-truths so that the women in the church would never find out that he was "dating" all of us.

What I ended up finding out was that he was dating me, the apostle, the young woman and another woman all at the same time and having us all as a part of his ministry while he was in Asbury Park, NJ. The apostle and the other woman caught on to what he was doing and left the ministry. The day when he was preaching that I mentioned earlier, when I said he stated to me about how he let it be known just because he didn't post about it didn't mean he was not in a relationship. Well, I found out by speaking to her and the other woman that was the same message he told them as well.

There was so much deception going on, and his armor bearer and musician knew everything that he was doing.

That's why the musician attempted to tell me the truth that one day, but I just didn't believe him. I believed this man when he stated everyone had turned against him, all the people he had helped. He was very good at playing the victim; it was always the fault of someone else and never his own doing. He never took ownership of anything that he had done to anyone. He literally had all three of us sitting in the church with him Sunday after Sunday until the other two left and it was just myself and the young woman left.

When he stopped holding services at the church in Asbury Park and moved the church to Newark, NJ on 6th Street, things were even crazier. It was on 6th Street where my friend and her family started to attend the church; even they could see something was off. However, everyone was so focused on God and transforming their lives, no one could focus on what brewing.

There were plenty of times where he squandered the church's money. I was coming out-of-pocket to either pay the full rent for the church or part of it. He had overdrawn the church's Chase bank account that was primarily in my name to the point where the account was closed. He was eventually evicted out of the church on 6th Street due to failure to maintain the rent.

When we moved to the church on Dodd Street in Bloomfield, he and I met with the pastor of that church; and he told the pastor about our relationship and that we were engaged to be married. The pastor offered for us to use his main sanctuary for our wedding and everything. So that pastor always called me First Lady, especially after we were married.

None of that stopped him though, no matter how many times he was caught, he would just keep going. I never knew why we couldn't go back to the church on Dodd Street. Once we moved to South Jersey, the money train of Nikiya had ran dry as I needed to ensure the rent was paid for our apartment. So once again he was asking me to find another church to rent out in Newark, which was how I located the church on Bergen Street. Lo and behold, the Bishop and his wife of the church on Bergen Street, actually knew his grandmother and remembered him from when he was a youth and would travel to that church with his grandmother.

So, when we met them, it was as if we were all family. We even told them when I discovered that I was pregnant. We literally had our first service at that church Easter Sunday 2018, which was the same day that we announced to the church that I was pregnant. Literally, no more than three days later, he was at the other church service with this young woman.

It was as if he had no reverence or respect for God, the people of God and the church. Until this very day, no one can tell me that he does. Often you see a meme going around that reads, "You're anointed until they don't like you anymore." That can be true. However, people like him, it truly makes me question was he ever really anointed. How one operates, how one truly believes, how one truly fears God, to me, comes into question when they absolutely fear no consequences.

What amazed me was how many people actually took the time out of their day and the breath in their body to defend him. He was a classic sociopathic narcissist, and he was being made to think that he was the victim.

There were so many times where he would state he was having a heart attack, and every other kind of attack known to man in order to get out of going somewhere in public with me. We were supposed to go to my spiritual parents' church anniversary together; and he didn't want to go because there was going to be a couple there that knew him. I was pregnant and showing, no matter how I tried to hide my stomach it was showing. He checked himself in to the hospital claiming he felt like he was having a heart attack; they discharged him and he told me he needed to rest, and for me to go to the banquet alone.

That following Sunday, I advised him that we needed to go to their church service since he missed the banquet and he obliged; and the same couple he was trying to avoid was right there, and the husband, a bishop was preaching. I will never forget that man, not knowing me at all, released a word to me and told him he better not hurt me. They made us hug in front of the church and everything. I will never forget my spiritual mother was looking, and afterwards, after everything happened and she and I spoke, she told me she felt that he didn't want to hug me.

How do you continue in a relationship with someone so devoid of loving themselves, let alone loving you? I had to figure out why I would ever stay in a relationship and suffer the way I did. And part of that lesson was I had to learn how to fall in love with myself again. Because if you cannot love yourself, you cannot love another person. The pain behind having a miscarriage and feeling alone, feeling tired, feeling broken had truly done its damage on my mental and emotional well-being; however, I had mastered the art of covering up how I felt.

To go through the biggest amount of deception and it was taking place in the church, in the place where I thought I was supposed to find refuge, peace, hope, and most of all love and protection; to see that I couldn't even feel safe in the "ark of safety" was detrimental to me. I stopped going to church; to me I could not trust a man-made structure or system that would not uphold its own beliefs and truths. For two years I refused to go to church regularly; I shut myself down in my house only interacting with those whom I felt I could trust, while shutting everyone else out.

I needed to find me, I needed to find my happiness, I needed to find my strength, my courage, my joy and my hope again. It all started when I decided to take the muzzle off and begin to speak. I encourage you to do the same. I have made mistakes that almost cost me my life, both naturally and spiritually. I learned how to love myself in the journey to heal.

Once I was granted the annulment on August 7, 2018 and I got the chance to start fresh as a restored woman, I finally felt a sense of freedom.

It wasn't until 2020 that I truly began to embrace the freedom and real love of self. It took Covid-19 to occur and for me to be forced in the house, quarantined without the ability to be around anyone for me to really begin becoming whole.

As I was forced in isolation, I began feeling signs of depression and anxiety; I was up all night, tired all day and snacking day and night. I was gaining weight and I knew I needed to deal with what was upsetting me.

The lack of trust I had for people grew, and I was still facing issues with even trusting my own self. When you go through a period of time with someone who constantly tells you that you are paranoid, making things up, it builds a cycle of distrusting your own voice, your own intuition. And I had grown to a place where I didn't even trust me; I didn't trust my ability to make decisions and I was unsure of myself.

I was watching myself get older and still not able to find true love, commitment, companionship, and partnership. To be thrown into a world pandemic and being alone was not helping.

I began to dwell on my miscarriage and the possibility of not being able to ever become a mother; I began to dwell on the fact that even in two years I was not able to secure a solid relationship with a man, heading towards marriage. I began to focus on everything that to me I was failing in, and I couldn't even see how far I had come.

I started to work out, I started to eat better, and I had a friend who showed me what it means to really be a friend, someone who would "keep" me; someone I could count on; and someone who would push me; and keep his word. He wasn't someone who was a talker, but rather a doer. That meant the most to me!

10

JOURNEY TO FREEDOM, FEARLESSLY!

⸘

With that I began to find my strength for real, and my voice started to be activated even the more, and I began to feel good on the inside, which it then began to show on the outside. In the midst of a pandemic, I found my purpose, and started a blog post and a podcast. I became a fearless storyteller and was no longer afraid of telling my story.

I was married to a man, to a bishop, in the church, who was married to three women at the same time. We became "The Secret Wives" unwillingly to a man that lied to us to bind us! We were and are three innocent women, who were caught in the web of a lying, manipulative, abusive, narcissistic almost sociopathic man who would do anything to keep his lies going because they fed his lifestyle. Someone with a huge ego, who needed his ego inflated by attention and the need to feel important and powerful, hence the "bishop" title but not in faith or in spirit.

I was strong enough to annul the marriage, keep my dignity, and not run from the issue that it happened.

However, even though I was a secret wife, that did not define who I am or was. Although I believed every lie, it didn't diminish my worth or my value, and because of that I can stand tall, ten toes down ready, willing, and able to live out my purpose.

I learned a great deal from then to now; I met that man in 2016, someone who was broken over death, who then became broken over a false marriage, who then found her strength, her value, her worth, her purpose and is living much better than she was and knowing that God is not done yet!!!

Even in the darkest of times, we must know that God is NOT DONE! It is not over!! You yet still have time to find YOU!!!

When you discover you, you unlock your unlimited potential, and you begin to live in PURPOSE!!!

Someone who was a secret wife, to become a bold, fearless, valuable woman who is a force to be reckoned with is the epitome of the strength of a woman!

I have learned to never live-in secrecy with anyone, if you are good enough to lay with, then you are good enough to be in public with. There is a big difference between private and secret; at times we confuse the two; however, secret is when in public you are not who you are in private.

Do not become the secret wife, the secret girlfriend, the secret friend or secret anything! You deserve more than a secret life!

I am Nikiya Mone, and I am not a secret! I am Nikiya Mone, and I live out loud, uninhibited, uncut, unadulterated, unfiltered with the muzzle of false religion, false faith, false belief, false doctrine, false self-view, false self-esteem REMOVED! Once the window shattered, everything shattered with it. FEAR LEFT and I became FEARLESS! YOU, TOO, CAN BECOME FEARLESS BY REMOVING THE MUZZLE AND SPEAKING TRUTH TO POWER. THIS IS NOT ABOUT TELLING YOUR TRUTH BUT LIVING IN TRUTH AND NOT ALLOWING ANYONE TO ALTER YOUR LIFE AND ALTER YOUR DESTINY. IT'S TIME TO LIVE A FULFILLED LIFE!

Printed in Great Britain
by Amazon